Supernatural Faith Disables

PREVIOUSLY PUBLISHED WITH
RESOURCE PUBLICATIONS

Nonfiction

Storms Are Faith's Workout: Preparing Christians for Spiritual Ambush (2018).
Faith's Journey Confronts Obstacles: Instructing God's Soldiers to Overcome in His Armor (2019).
Satan's Strategy to Torment Through Physical Ambush: Educating God's Soldiers of Satan's Plot to Shatter Faith through Sickness and Disease (2019).
Spiritual Shipwreck on the Horizon: Exhorting Christians to Contend for the Faith and Comprehend the Deceitfulness of Sin (2019).
Satan Has No Authority Over God's Soldier: Illuminating Godlike Faith (2019).
God: The Holy Spirit: The Conquering Power Within (2019).
Signs of the Time: Warning: Lukewarm Christianity Accepts Deception (2020)
Flesh and Spirit Conflict: The Inner Battle of Choice (2020).

Fiction

The Elfdins and the Gold Temple: An Oralee Chronicle (2018).
Charlie McGee and the Leprechaun: Life's Curious Twist of Events (2019).
The Shrines of Manitoba: Dark Secrets Shall Be Brought to Light (2019).
Guilty As Blood: One Can Make a Difference (2019).
Back From the Dead: Light Shines As the Noonday Sun (2020).
Nazis, Holocaust, and Self-Love: Unbridled Bigotry (2020).
Chateau de Paix: Nightmare Hiding In Paradise (2020).

Supernatural Faith Disables

Quench the Fiery Darts

R. C. JETTE

RESOURCE *Publications* • Eugene, Oregon

SUPERNATURAL FAITH DISABLES
Quench the Fiery Darts

Resource Publications
An Imprint of Wipf and Stock Publishers
199 W. 8th Ave., Suite 3
Eugene, OR 97401

www.wipfandstock.com

PAPERBACK ISBN: 978-1-7252-8454-8
HARDCOVER ISBN: 978-1-7252-8455-5
EBOOK ISBN: 978-1-7252-8456-2

Manufactured in the U.S.A.   08/24/20

This book is dedicated to my Lord Jesus Christ
who makes the impossible possible by faith.

To my husband (Paul)
who has been by my side through thick and thin.

My son (PJ) his daughter (Kierra), my daughter (Dawn) who
has freed me up to write, my daughter (Christina) her sons
(Andrew, Matthew, Joshua) and her daughter (Sarah)
who is with the Lord.

Susanna and Mike who have been such a help,
and to all who have influenced my life throughout the years.

My special thanks is given to Wipf and Stock Publishers
for their continued publication of my books
under their Resource Publications.

I thank Joe Delahanty, Jim Tedrick, Joshua Little,
Ian Creeger, and Stephanie Randels.

Special mention is given to Matthew Wimer, George Callihan,
Shannon Carter, and Savanah N. Landerholm to whom words
cannot convey my gratitude.

For whatsoever is born of God overcometh the world:
and this is the victory that overcometh the world, even our faith.
(1 John 5:4)

Above all, taking the shield of Faith, wherewith ye shall be able to
quench all the fiery darts of the wicked.
(Ephesians 6:16)

Bless the Lord, O my soul, and forget not all his benefits;
Who forgiveth all thine iniquities; who healeth all thy diseases;
Who redeemeth thy life from destruction;
who crowneth thee with lovingkindness and tender mercies;
Who satisfieth thy mouth with good things;
so that thy youth is renewed like the eagle's.
(Psalm 103:1–5)

Contents

Introduction

I BELIEVE THERE ARE times that seeing things from a different perspective helps illuminate what was not understood before. It appears God's soldiers are becoming weary in the constant warfare against our bodies and are battling with our faith. Our once stable foundation has begun to crumble under our feet. Physical sickness, disease, ill-health has weakened our resolve and we question if healing really belongs to God's soldiers.

In this book, I will endeavor to use different aspects of faith to encourage the downtrodden to rise above whatever storm or fiery dart of Satan trying to engulf them. Whether we are facing sin, sickness, grief, financial difficulty, etc., it is the same principle of faith to disable the fiery darts.

If the faith walk was a walk in the park, God would not have emphasized that only he that *overcometh* shall inherit all things; and I will be his God, and he shall be my son (Revelation 21:7). We are at war with a supernatural enemy bent on our destruction. Only supernatural weapons will defeat him.

I revealed in my first book *Storms Are Faith's Workout* the importance of comprehending that storms are to be expected if we are to live by faith. Storms happen as surely as the sun rises and sets each day. Yet, many of God's soldiers are ill prepared for the storms that assail us almost daily. Unless we comprehend what Christ's death on the cross has given us, we will keep being overcome by the storms, obstacles, and strategies the devil hurls at us.

As we look around, we see some people overcoming whatever storm is flung at them, while others are being overcome by the storm. The severity of the storm is not the question, the question is why do some overcome, and others go under?

The Bible is quite explicit that God is not a respecter of persons (Romans (9:6). So, what makes the difference? Do others possess something different? I believe it's because many Christians do not know how to use the faith God has given them. It's like the person who has a typewriter, but has never learned to type. We can't blame the typewriter for our inefficiency and incompetence in our inability to type. Likewise, we can't blame God for our inefficiency and incompetence in our ability to be men and women of supernatural faith.

God has dealt to each of us a measure of faith (Romans 12:3). God desires that we truly represent Christ by overcoming daily. God's soldiers are supposed to be children of faith. We should see healings and miracles take place. A natural faith will not succeed or triumph. We must understand for faith to work, it has to be on the supernatural level. It must rise from the natural to the supernatural. It must rise from the physical to the spiritual.

Christian, when we were born again, the measure of faith we received was and still is enough to overcome everything we will ever face. That measure of faith is able to move mountains out of our life. It is able to heal. It is able to get our bills paid. It is able to give us the victory in whatever storm, obstacle, strategy of Satan comes our way.

This book is meant to enlighten God's soldiers about supernatural faith and its power to quench the fiery darts of Satan. No matter what we may have to confront on our journey of faith, supernatural faith will disable it.

Although we should come away with the knowledge to disable or quench all the fiery darts of Satan, we should attain an understanding of how to overcome the fiery darts that are aimed at our physical body. A proper knowledge will defeat unbelief.

My book, *Satan's Strategy to Torment Through Physical Ambush: Educating God's Soldiers of Satan's Plot to Shatter Faith Through Sickness and Disease*, was written to enlighten God's soldiers to the satanic stronghold that has developed against the Body of Christ.

Prayerfully, in these pages supernatural faith to quench all fiery darts, as well as disabling the darts of sickness and disease will be revealed. It has become apparent that many are losing the battle to fight demonic attacks in our bodies. When that happens, we lose many other battles.

In the book mentioned above, I revealed Satan's strategy to physically ambush God's soldiers. If you have not read it, I recommend it as a foundation for this book. The devil knows that we seem to be the weakest when we are fighting sickness and disability in our own bodies. We become self-centered and often become oblivious to what is going on around us. This is made evident on the battle field during any war. Once a soldier is injured, he/she can lose focus on the battle because of the severity of the injury.

It can be difficult to focus on the needs of others while we are tending to our pain, sickness, disease, grief, difficulties, troubles, etc. That's why we must comprehend that Satan is working overtime to get God's soldiers mindful of our own problems, our own storms, our own mountains, our own obstacles, our own bodily affliction, etc.

Healing is the children's bread. Jesus made that truth clear in his discourse with the woman from Canaan. He made evident that healing belongs to God's soldiers (his children). As long as we know that God is NOT calling us home, it is his will for us to be in health.

I stated in my book, *Satan's Strategy to Torment Through Physical Ambush*, the only time we may have to endure a sickness or disease is because God has permitted a thorn in our flesh to keep us humble. However, I also revealed that a thorn in the flesh, allowed by God, will manifest the power of God in our life. This is seen in the lives of the Apostle Paul, Joni Eareckson Tada, as well as others such as Nicholas James Vujicic an Australian Christian evangelist who was born without arms and legs. Each life exhibits or exhibited the power of God in a mighty way. Despite the infirmity, they reveal what a vessel yielded to God can do.

In other words, if our infirmity continuously keeps us from doing what God has called us to do, it is NOT a thorn in our flesh. It is a strategy of Satan to keep us incapacitated, debilitated, weakened, out of action, etc. and must be disabled through faith. We must learn to quench the fiery darts through supernatural faith.

If you have picked up this book, you are seeking the where-with to overcome the battle raging in your body. Whether you are trying to overcome sin, sickness, disease, etc., this book is meant to reinforce the truth that supernatural faith resides in you through the Holy Spirit. That faith or power is able to quench all the fiery darts assailed against you, and enable you to receive spiritual and physical healing!

Chapter 1

The Conference Table

Come now, and let us reason together, saith the Lord:
though your sins be as scarlet, they shall be as white as
snow; though they be red like crimson, they shall be
as wool. If ye be willing and obedient, ye shall eat the
good of the land: But if ye refuse and rebel, ye shall be
devoured with the sword: for the mouth of the Lord hath
spoken it (Isaiah 1:18–20).

BEFORE WE CAN COMPREHEND what supernatural faith is capable of, we first have to ascertain if we are in a right relationship with God. We can't be in some sort of sin, unbelief, or doubt and believe we can disable or quench fiery darts. It's imperative we understand the significance of the conference table before we are enabled to walk in supernatural faith that disables the enemy's tactics.

We usually relate these verses in Isaiah with a salvation message. Although salvation begins at the conference table, for this book, we must comprehend that God is talking to his children in the scripture text. He is bidding us to come to the table and be made clean of our unbelief, our doubt, our sin stain.

Once we realize what the Lord is saying, we are motivated by its beauty. We feel beckoned like a refreshing dip in the pool on a hot and humid day. I believe too many are forgetting or have forgotten the beauty of God's word. This scripture should humble and inspire us at its meaning.

Yet, much of God's word is taken in a superficial manner going in one ear and out the other. Once we understand what Isaiah is saying to God's soldiers, we will stand in awe and fall to our knees at its implication.

Do we comprehend that our sin stains are so bright and revealing, and yet we are called to the conference table with God? Christians who choose of our own free-will to rebel against our savior, who choose to ignore God and go our own way, who choose to not believe his word, who allow false teaching to instigate our faith, who blatantly turn our back on God are called to his conference table.

Through all our rebellion, God is extending compassion and grace. By rights, a meeting, a pleading for mercy should come from the offending party. We are the ones who have offended God. Yet, He is calling us to come to his conference table.

Any time we choose a way contrary to God, we will get hurt. If we travel the wrong way on a major highway, we will most likely get killed if not seriously injured. Yet, why do God's soldiers, time and again insist on being hearers and not doers of his word and become deceived? (James 1:22). Why do we not heed his word? Why do we claim to love God and keep not his word or commandments? Jesus makes clear that if we love him, we will keep his commandments (John 14:15).

Why do we hear his word and not do it? It's simple. We really love self and choose what "I" want. We cannot decide to obey the Word of God that suits us and disobey what we don't like. Why are we so bent on refusing to heed God's word that is full of warning signs exposing danger if we take a wrong turn?

It seems to be a vicious cycle of ignoring God's word and getting hurt. Then we blame God. The word of warning or caution signs were there, but we chose to ignore them because they went against what we wanted to do. We decided that self had precedence over God's word and blatantly disobeyed. We preferred to be a hearer only and not a doer of the word.

The sad reality is that when we get hurt, we accuse God. We point a finger at him and say, "I trusted you, and you failed me." Or we say, "I prayed for your will. Why am I in this predicament?" Through our own choices, we allow ourselves to miss out on God's blessings promised for obedience. We were a hearer only and blame God for reaping what we sowed. His word is unchangeable. If we sow something, we can't expect to reap or harvest something different (Galatians 6:7). Disobedience to God's word will reap chastisement or punishment. Obedience to God's word will reap his promises.

Let me give an example. A woman I knew was dating and about to marry a non-Christian. She was allowing him to smoke and drink in her house. I gave her the Scriptures about not being unequally yoked together with unbelievers (2 Corinthians 6:14). I tried to warn her that if she married him, she would have Satan as her father-in-law. The devil's kid can only act like the devil. Anyway, she became angry and quoted scriptures back to me.

1. Love covers a multitude of sins (1 Peter 4:8).
2. How shall they hear without a preacher (Romans 10:14).
3. For God is love (1 John 4:8).

I explained the love we are to have is loving enough to tell the truth that will keep them from going to Hell. That means telling them the reality of their sinful condition and hopefully bringing them to repentance. God doesn't want his children to love the lost in a carnal way that dates them, marries them, fellowships with them, goes into business with them, etc. in deliberate disobedience to his word.

After she married, he was drunk most of the time and physically abused her. When he became tired of her, he left her for someone else. She deserted the Lord for a while claiming she prayed for his will. It took time, but she repented of choosing her will and not God's. His will was clear in his word, but she ignored God's word about being yoked with unbelievers and the signs of his intoxication to satisfy what she wanted. The moment she chose to be a hearer and not doer, she gave place to be deceived (James 1:22).

We can't claim to be praying for God's will when we are a hearer only of his word. His word says to not be unequally yoked with unbelievers. How can we claim to pray for his will when his will is clearly stated in his word?

I don't know how many times I have been told by Christians, "My situation is different, those scriptures don't apply to me." How ridiculous is that statement? We are driving down the street and see a sign "Bridge Out—Detour" and we decide it doesn't apply to me. We drive on.

Do we think our car will fly over the danger? How ridiculous to think we can continue on the path and ignore the warning signs. We will pay some serious consequences.

Man ignoring God's word is not a new thing. It started in the Garden of Eden. Just as the Fall of Man caused hurt and pain, our falling today will cause hurt and pain. When we find ourselves in such circumstances because of disobedience, we hold a grudge against God for our actions. Until we admit it was me and not God, we believe we can't trust him, and our faith walk is hindered.

Now, even though we're holding a grudge against God, He still calls us to the conference table. In all that we do to hurt, offend, blame God, etc., He still calls us to a meeting to straighten out our mess. God didn't make this mess, we made it of our own free-will.

Do we comprehend what God is saying to us in Isaiah 1:18? Do we realize the one who possesses all power and in a single moment could crush or destroy his offenders, those who have ignored his word, are called to meet him at his conference table?

How can God who has been so offended by our sin call us to a conference table? He is moved by his love and mercy. Think about that. We are guilty and have committed a crime against God, yet He is willing to not only drop all the charges but to cleanse us, to reconcile us, and to deliver us from the mess we got ourselves into.

God doesn't want to condemn and destroy his people. He offers the conference table to give us an opportunity to receive full forgiveness and complete pardon when we repent. To repent means that we change our mind (we admit the error of our way and turn away from our sin). God's forgiveness is available the moment we confess our sins, repent, and accept spiritual cleansing through the blood of Jesus Christ (1 John 1:7–9).

Any time we have a deep stain on something, it is essentially impossible to eradicate. The stain of our sin is equally permanent. But God promises if we meet him at the conference table, the blood of Christ will remove the stain from our life. There is no excuse to continue perpetually stained. If we are willing and obedient, Christ will forgive us and remove the most deep-rooted, the most engrained, the most embedded stain from our life.

When we became born again, we met at the conference table. Now, the conference table is not a one-time meeting. Even after we are saved, there are times we will choose to ignore God's word. We will find ourselves not denying self and being out of God's will.

That's why God calls us to his conference table. He knows that we fail, but He doesn't want us to stay down. If we fall, we will not be utterly rejected. The Lord will uphold us with his hand (Psalms 37:23–24). God is ever there to help his child who stumbles and beckoning us back to a right relationship with him.

> Let us therefore come boldly unto the throne of grace,
> that we may obtain mercy, and find grace to help in time
> of need (Hebrews 4:16).

No matter how great or how small the wrong, the sin, the injury against God is, go to the conference table (the throne of grace) immediately. It is immediately accessible to us the moment we realize we have sinned against his word. There is no waiting line. God is there waiting for us.

> And he said, A certain man had two sons: And the younger of them said to his father, Father, give me the portion of goods that falleth to me. And he divided unto them his living. And not many days after the younger son gathered all together, and took his journey into a far country, and there wasted his substance with riotous living . . . And when he came to himself , he said, How many hired servants of my father's have bread enough and to spare, and I perish with hunger! I will arise and go to my father, and will say unto him, Father, I have sinned against heaven, and before thee, And am no more worthy to be called thy son . . . But when he was yet a great way

off, his father saw him, and had compassion, and ran, and fell on his neck, and kissed him (Luke 15:11–20).

That is what our heavenly Father does when He sees us coming towards the conference table. He is not standing there with a whip in his hand ready to beat us for our sins. When we repent, He is there with open arms welcoming us back into his fellowship. There is no love as forgiving than that of our God who gave his life for this relationship.

If we are a Christian and have found ourselves in a situation because of sin, we must understand we ignored or disobeyed the warning in his word. If we can't understand why God didn't stop something from happening, guaranteed, we ignored his word. We heard, but we didn't do. We allowed ourselves to be deceived. We were where we shouldn't have been. We did what we shouldn't have done. We yoked up with unbelievers. We believed a lie and ignored the truth.

We have to admit in our heart that it was me and not God. Once we admit we sinned against God, we receive an inner peace. Until we admit from our heart that we sinned, we will continue to blame God for not stopping us and not preventing it from happening. His word makes clear that we have been given a free-will. God can't stop us from doing what we willfully choose to do. A free-will means it's our choice. We choose to obey God's will or our will. God doesn't tempt us to sin, we sin when we allow sin to entice us and yield to it (James 1:13–15).

Faith welcomes the conference table. What do I mean by that? We realize we must always go there to be reconciled with God for disobeying his word, for disbelief, or for going our own way. Faith knows that if we meet God at the conference table, He will forgive us, deliver us, and cleanse us. Our stain is washed as white as snow!

Chapter 2

Supernatural Faith Is Not Natural

> Now faith is the substance of things hoped for, the evidence of things not seen. Through faith, we understand that the worlds were framed by the word of God, so that things which are seen were not made of things which do appear (Hebrews 11:1,3).

IN THIS CHAPTER, I will bring forth some truths I have stated in previous books. Although it will repeat previously declared facts, it will be adding and clarifying God-like faith. I believe it is necessary for us to grasp the truth of God's faith in order to allow supernatural faith that disables whatever storm, obstacle, strategy Satan hurls our way to be empowered in our life.

Faith is not natural, but supernatural. It is not a physical attribute but a spiritual characteristic. In order to comprehend that faith is supernatural, we must realize that God is the author or creator of faith. Faith is an attribute of God. Supernatural faith is not part of the natural creation. It resides in the supernatural or spiritual realm of God.

Genesis chapter one informs us that God spoke all things into existence by his word. He said, "Let there be," and it was. Then in Hebrews 11:3, we learn that God caused to exist what did not previously exist before the moment He called them into existence. All God created was not created out of anything that existed before He said, "Let there be." When He spoke, what was not visible appeared or materialized.

God, by his faith, through his word spoken, brought into being all that which did not exist before He called it forth. In other words, God took faith and made the worlds. Faith was his substance to create all things.

If we are to walk in supernatural faith, we must understand that faith originated in God. As I have taught before, we must recognize that there are two worlds. There is the supernatural, spiritual, invisible world, and the natural, physical, visible world.

In my book, *Faith's Journey Confronts Obstacles*, I revealed that in order for faith to work, we must recognize that there are two worlds—the spiritual, invisible world and the natural, physical visible world. Faith will not work if we don't comprehend one is natural or fleshly and the other is supernatural or spiritual. To overcome by faith, we must separate the natural world from the spiritual world.

Because faith originated in God, it is of the supernatural world. Supernatural, disabling, or overcoming faith is not found in the natural world. We use the word faith so lightly. We claim to have faith in someone or something. But that faith is based on man's wisdom, knowledge, understanding, ability, power, etc.

Supernatural faith or the faith of God has nothing to do with the natural or physical realm. It generates from the supernatural or spiritual realm. It is based on God's wisdom, knowledge, understanding, ability, power, etc. We must understand that faith is a superseding force that existed before the natural world existed. Hebrews 11:3 makes clear that the word of God framed the worlds through faith.

God created everything we see through or by his faith. Supernatural faith is an attribute of God and we who have the Holy Spirit residing in us are partakers of that attribute. We don't have to seek faith, it resides in us.

Let me explain what I mean. When we were born physically, we were born with a brain. It would be silly for me to pray for a brain when it is part of my human birth. We have natural or humanistic qualities from our human parents.

Once we have our spiritual birth, we receive spiritual qualities from our spiritual Father. Yet how many Christians pray for God to give them faith, to give them love, to give them peace, to give them temperance or self-control, etc. When God gave us those qualities when we were born again. They are fruit of the Spirit (Galatians 5:22–23). If we are born again, we have God's attributes of faith, love, peace, self-control, etc. residing in us. It's not God's fault if we don't cultivate those attributes.

Let me explain, if we have a garden and allow the weeds, insects, rodents, etc. to overrun our garden, we will have no fruit. It's imperative that we comprehend that anything that is opposite of God's word is a weed, insect, rodent, etc. that will destroy the fruit of the Holy Spirit.

When we were born of man, God gave us what we needed to live in this world. Whatever we needed to live in this natural life, we were born with. Some may say, what about those born blind, deaf, or whatever? I think of Helen Keller who was born deaf and blind, but went on to earn a Bachelor of Arts degree. She was an author, lecturer, etc. She didn't look at her lack, but saw her God-given potential and overcame. An incredible example is Nicholas James Vujicic, the Australian Evangelist who was born without arms or legs. Yet, God has empowered him to witness around the world.

Now, when we were born of God, He gave us whatever we needed to live a spiritual, overcoming, victorious life. We lack nothing spiritually to walk in supernatural faith that enables us to disable and quench every fiery dart of the devil. If we are not overcoming, it's because we are not using what we've received.

What do I mean? It's simple. If I have a bicycle sitting in my garage, I can't complain that I don't know how to ride it. I have to get on that bike and pedal until I become proficient on it. Yes, I may fall and be injured. But after a while, riding will be so automatic that I don't even think about staying up.

As we walk in the Spirit, we will be performing things through supernatural faith instinctively. It's only when we allow the flesh to rule us, that faith becomes an incredible effort. There is no God-like faith in our physical man. Supernatural or God-like faith resides in our spiritual man.

Faith is believing we have something before we get it even though there is no physical evidence (Hebrews 11:1). Let's understand this truth. If we ask God for $1,000, we may believe we have it by faith, but our wallet is empty. We may ask God to heal us, and by faith we believe we are healed, but the pain is still there. The natural facts say our wallet is empty and the pain is still there, but by faith the money is in our wallet, and the pain is gone.

Faith is a spiritual truth, so we believe the money is there in the spirit world—in the mind of God. Therefore, in the faith world, in the mind of God, the money is in our wallet. However, when we look in our wallet, it's not there. What are we going to believe? Do we believe fact, or do we believe faith? If we believe fact, our wallet will stay empty. If we believe faith, in the fulness of his time, the money will be in our wallet. Likewise, if we believe fact, the pain will remain. If we believe faith, in the fulness of his time, the pain will be gone.

It's time for God's soldiers to shake off unbelief like the Apostle Paul did with the viper in Acts 28:5. If we allow unbelief to get a firm grip on our faith, we will succumb to its poisonous venom. Believe me, unbelief or doubt will endeavor to attach itself to us, but we decide if it does or doesn't. We have the choice to shake it off or allow it to attach itself to us.

Since supernatural faith is not part of the natural realm, it will not work unless we learn to separate the two realms. We have to comprehend faith is the dominant force that existed before God created the natural world. How do we know that? We know that God created the world, the sun, the moon, the stars through his faith. Thus, faith existed before the worlds.

If it was here before the natural world, it is part of the supernatural realm of God. Faith is not part of this natural, physical world. We must view faith as a supernatural, spiritual realism separate from the natural.

We must stop trying to make faith part of the physical realm when it's part of the spiritual realm. Faith is not part of man's knowledge, man's logic, man's wisdom, man's science, man's medicine, or man's ability.

Faith is not a physical component, it is a spiritual component. It began in eternity past with God. It is a characteristic quality of God. Since God is a spiritual, eternal being, faith is an eternal force of the spiritual realm.

Faith began in God who is perfect. Therefore, his faith is perfect. There are no defects, flaws, deficiencies, shortcomings, etc. in God's faith. Once the revelation of God's faith permeates our being, it will revolutionize our faith. It will transform our faith walk to one that overcomes all storms, obstacles, temptation, etc.

God's creating all things by faith through his word is not like a potter molding his clay into something. The clay is here for the potter to use. God had nothing but his faith to create the physical worlds. There was nothing in the physical world for him to use.

> I have declared the former things from the beginning,
> and they went forth out of my mouth, and I shewed them;
> I did them suddenly, and they came to pass (Isaiah 48:3).

Isaiah is saying that God created things suddenly. In other words, as the words came out of his mouth, things were immediately made visible.

Hebrews 11:1 tells us that faith is the substance of things hoped for, the evidence of things not seen. What is that saying? It is informing us that faith is the substance or foundation for something to stand on. That which we can hold onto. It takes faith to get substance. As we understand this truth, we will be enabled to confront all storms, trials, etc. and overcome them by faith.

God's faith was the substance that enabled him to speak forth and create. His faith was the substance or foundation on which He created (spoke) all things into existence. He believed and brought forth. When God spoke the word or the words came forth out of his mouth, something that never existed was created from nothing physical.

God's soldiers have to realize that God can do the impossible because He has no unbelief, no doubt, no alloyed faith in his ability.

His character contains no unbelief or doubt. As God is love, God is holy, God is faith, etc.

There is nothing impossible with God (Luke 1:37). God is capable of doing what may seem impossible to us. There is nothing beyond the scope of his power. That's why when we expect God to do whatever He says, He will do it (Hebrews 11:6). No power can hinder or stop him.

His supernatural faith is present everywhere, knows everything, can never change, and has unlimited power. Nothing hinders God's supernatural faith. Only our unbelief hinders his working in our life. We doubt, we waiver, we yield to our flesh and not to the Spirit. When we walk in the Spirit, God's supernatural faith performs the impossible.

God is a Spirit being. He is eternal. When Genesis 1:1 stated *in the beginning*, it didn't mean the beginning of God. God is eternal and eternity goes forever in both directions of past and future. The beginning in Genesis refers to the beginning of time. Time started when God created the physical worlds.

Faith is part of eternity because it was here before creation. Its author or creator is God who is the beginning and the ending of all things. He has always been here and will always be here. Faith is supernatural and spiritual like God.

We must not base our faith on our faith, our ability, or our power. Supernatural faith is based on God's faith, God's ability, and God's power. It's not faith in our faith, but it's faith in God, his word, his ability, and his power.

It's God who brings forth what we believe him to do. It is God who brought forth our salvation when we believed him to do it. It is God who brings forth his promises when we believe him to do it. We need to learn to believe in his faith, his power, his ability to do whatever He says.

I've given this example before, but I believe it reveals what happens when supernatural faith is exhibited. What God's faith can do when we believe him.

My husband was remodeling an old house in Connecticut, while we lived in it. It was a trying period without a kitchen for some time. Anyway, carpenter ants had eaten away the timber sill on a stone foundation under the kitchen. The beam was eight inches by eight inches in diameter and ten or more feet long.

We were short on money, so Paul was in the basement using hydraulic jacks to lift-up the house while attempting to force the new beam into place after he had cleaned out the old one. Let me explain that the house was three stories high. No matter what he did, he could not get the house to lift in order to move the new beam into place.

This went on for a couple of days, and he was quite frustrated. As I was praying, I sensed the Lord wanted me to go upstairs and stand at the place in the kitchen where the beam needed to go under. As I stood there, the Lord told me his armor was in place and to pray. I prayed and told the Lord I knew He had the power to do anything. Then I said, "Father, only you can perform the miracle that is needed here. You are our God, and nothing is impossible with you. We have no money to hire anyone to jack up the house." I then stretched forth my hands over the spot and said. "In the Name of Jesus, show my husband the power of the God he serves."

The next thing I knew is that the whole house along with me was lifted up, and I heard this loud noise. I got my bearings and ran down to the basement, found the hydraulic jacks on the floor, Paul and our daughter, Dawn, standing away from the spot with mouths open and eyes widened. My husband just stood dumbfounded, but Dawn said, "Mom, the house lifted up, and the beam went into place by itself. Dad was trying to push it in and fell forwards as the beam went into place by itself." I looked at my husband who shook his head and said, "Just before the house lifted and the beam went into place, the Lord said to my heart, "You underestimate the power of your God." I then told them both what the Lord had me do.

Once we grasp hold of what God's faith can do, we don't doubt any promise He gives us. Too many of God's soldiers do err, not knowing the scriptures, nor the power of God (Matthew 22:29). Only the supernatural faith of God can lift up a three-story house.

If we want to walk in the faith that overcomes, we must comprehend that faith is supernatural. It's God's faith, God's power, God's ability that spoke the worlds into existence. He spoke from the spiritual world and the physical world appeared the moment He spoke it into being. It has not changed, He speaks from the spiritual world to manifest or bring about our promise, our answered prayer, etc. into the physical or natural world.

God will never change, He is the same yesterday, today, and forever (Hebrews 13:8). Understanding that truth enables us to believe that when He promises something, even if it seems impossible, we don't look at the physical or natural. We look at God and his attributes, and we believe in his supernatural ability and power to perform whatever He promises.

We must realize that supernatural faith is believing in God's faith that can do anything. He has the faith to believe what seems impossible in the natural realm. He created all the physical realm by his word through faith. Why do we doubt that He can bring our promise from the spiritual realm into the physical realm?

Once we comprehend God's faith can do the impossible, we know that we can face any hardship, trial, storm, etc. We will disable anything contrary to God by confronting it and overcoming it in the supernatural faith, power, and ability of our God who created all the physical worlds by his faith!

Chapter 3

Supernatural Armor Is Not Physical

10) Finally, my brethren, be strong in the Lord, and in the power of his might. 11) Put on the whole armour of God, that ye may be able to stand against the wiles of the devil. 12) For we wrestle not against flesh and blood, but against principalities, against powers, against the rulers of the darkness of this world, against spiritual wickedness in high places. 13) Wherefore take unto you the whole armour of God; that ye may be able to withstand in the evil day, and having done all, to stand. 14) Stand therefore, having your loins girt about with truth, and having on the breastplate of righteousness; 15) And your feet shod with the preparation of the gospel of peace; 16) Above all, taking the shield of faith, wherewith ye shall be able to quench all the fiery darts of the wicked. 17) And take the helmet of salvation, and the sword of the Spirit, which is the word of God: 18) Praying always with all prayer and supplication in the Spirit, and watching thereunto with all perseverance and supplication for all saints. (Ephesians 6:10–18)

FOR A FULLER COMPREHENSION of God's supernatural armor, I suggest reading my book *Faith's Journey Confronts Obstacles: Instructing God's Soldiers to Overcome in His Armor*. That book will lay the foundation permitting this book to enlighten more perfectly God's armor.

This chapter on supernatural armor is meant to build on the fact that supernatural faith disables or quenches the fiery darts of the devil. If we are to walk in supernatural faith, we have to be dressed in faith's supernatural armor. Neither one are part of the natural or physical realm. They are elements of God's supernatural or spiritual realm.

We understand that armor is the metal coverings formerly worn by soldiers or warriors to protect the body in battle. Of this armor, we've all seen pictures of knights going to battle. Soldiers did not go into battle without their armor.

However, our supernatural armor is invisible. But without a knowledge or understanding of how it works or protects, we have lost the battle before we start.

Our supernatural or God's armor is not the first outfit that many of God's soldiers put on when going to war. We are fleshly and revert to natural means when confronted with a battle. We need to comprehend that we do not confront a natural enemy, but a supernatural enemy.

Whenever we confront a supernatural enemy in our flesh, we will lose the battle. If we confront in the supernatural armor of God, we will disable the enemy's fiery darts or weapons. Putting on our supernatural armor should be as natural as getting dressed.

Ephesians 6:10 is commanding or directing us to be strong in the Lord, and in the power of his might. We are to be empowered through the supreme in authority, to be increased in strength through God and in the ability of his strength.

Supernatural faith happens when we are empowered through our union with Christ and draw our strength from the power and ability of God's strength. Our strength is not drawn from physical strength, but from God's supernatural strength that is unlimited, unrestrained, and boundless.

SUPERNATURAL ARMOR IS NOT PHYSICAL

We have no supernatural ability in our flesh, for it is a spiritual power. Supernatural ability comes from our supernatural God.

Ephesians 6:11 tells us to put on the whole armor of God. We are to array with, clothe with, *endue* with. If we are to be enabled to stand against the wiles of the devil, we must be endued with God's supernatural armor.

We are to stand erect like a tree with its roots deep into the ground and the violent storms have no effect on it. Thus, when the devil comes at us with his wiles, his methods, his trickery, his fiery darts, we are not uprooted.

We must comprehend the devil is a predator waiting to catch us without our armor and attack. Satan waits for that weak moment, whatever it may be, and strikes. It is crucial that we learn how to use our supernatural armor. If the devil can get us in our flesh, he will beat us. We cannot battle in the natural against a supernatural enemy.

This command must be understood. We are commanded or ordered by our God to put on his supernatural armor. That means we are to dress, clothe, array ourselves in his full armor. God has supplied the armor, the putting on is our responsibility. He will not dress us. If we neglect his supernatural armor, it's not his fault if we lose a battle.

Let me explain, when my children were young, I used to lay out their clothes the night before. They were old enough to dress themselves. All they had to do was put on what I had ready for them. That's the way it is with the supernatural armor of God. He has everything ready for us, but we must put it on. Only as we clothe ourselves in his supernatural armor, that He has supplied, will we be able to stand in supernatural faith and disable or quench the fiery darts of the devil.

Ephesians 6:12 is educating us to the fact that we do not fight against flesh and blood. We are not opposing human or physical adversaries of the natural realm. We fight against principalities, against supernatural forces, powers, armies, or influences. We fight against the rulers of the darkness of this world that have the qualities and attributes of Satan. We fight against spiritual wickedness meaning supernatural and demonic malice, plots, and strategies in high places (the heavenlies or supernatural, spiritual realm).

Our fight is not against physical or natural barriers, they are supernatural, spiritual, and invisible to our naked eye. We fight the demonic spirits behind or controlling those who oppose us. Demonic plots or strategies are being planned in the supernatural realm and are carried out through those manipulated by Satan in the natural realm. It looks like people, but it is not. The person or persons are activated by demonic forces that have power over them. Remember Satan can take captive his followers at his will (2 Timothy 2:26).

This truth is made evident by what is happening around us. Look at all the hostility, hate, malice that has recently manifested. That's why we must never react in our flesh or we will be powerless against the demonic power operating or controlling the person or the mob.

Ephesians 6:13 tells us the whole armor of God will enable us to withstand in the evil day. That means the armor gives what is necessary to stand against, to resist, or to oppose. If we have done all, we have worked out all things. Again, we're told to take unto or put on the whole armor that God supplies. Only in his full armor can we stand against, resist, oppose the devil's plots, malice, disease, etc. However, the key in withstanding is *having done all*. It means that we have worked out everything. We know how to put on the armor and are proficient in its use. We have proved or verified it.

In 1 Samuel chapter seventeen, when Saul wanted David to use his armor, David refused. He had not verified or proved Saul's armor. He did not know if he could trust or rely on it. David used what he knew and had proven. He used God's armor. Of course, Goliath laughed at him because he saw a young lad standing without armor. God's armor is invisible to the naked eye for it is not physical but spiritual.

The devil knows if God's soldiers are clothed in God's armor or in our flesh. When he sees the armor of God, he knows he cannot overcome us unless he deceives or dupes us. He tries to persuade us to believe an evil report that we have no chance against what we are fighting. It's hopeless, etc.

In my Christian fiction book *The Elfdins and the Gold Temple*, is shown how the devil through his follower deceived the Elfdins into thinking they had no power against him. They fell into four-hundred years of a dark age because of the enemy's deception.

God tells us if we put on his armor and stand, we will withstand, survive, resist, recognize, disable, quench, and overcome whatever the devil hurls our way.

Ephesians 6:14 begins to introduce the armor. We are to stand, be erect, upright, vertical, while girt with truth void of lies or falsehoods. God's soldiers are to stand in or with the truth of God and his word. The breastplate of righteousness implies covering the chest, lungs, heart which are needed for life.

When we are girt with the truth of God's word, we discover, we recognize, we see who our enemies are and how they come at us to attack. It is through the word of God that we recognize false doctrines, false beliefs, lies, deceptions, etc. With the recognition of these, we see where the enemy's snares are waiting to trip us up. That's why it's so imperative to study and know God's word. If we do not know the truth of what He says, we can be easily led astray by false doctrines, wolves in sheep's clothing, self-deception, etc.

Now, the heart of man is the seat of his affections, loyalties, desires, etc. All our affections, loyalties, and desires stem or center in our heart. The breastplate of righteousness is, in fact, the life of God in the soul. Righteousness in our heart defines or determines everything on which our spiritual existence depends. The breastplate of righteousness defends the lungs and the heart. This indicates the heart's affections upon which spiritual life depends. Let me explain. If our heart's affection is centered upon some sort of sin, unrighteousness defines our heart. Whereas, if our heart's affection is centered upon holiness and godliness, righteousness defines our heart.

If our heart stops beating and we no longer breathe, we are dead. Well, righteousness determines our spiritual life. Without righteousness, there is no spiritual life. In other words, we are spiritually dead. The breastplate of righteousness is meant to protect our spiritual life from the attacks of the enemy.

God's soldiers need to realize the importance of righteousness. The crown of righteousness is only attained by fighting the good fight, finishing our course, and keeping the faith (2 Timothy 4:7–8). A prayer of salvation doesn't determine our spiritual life, a life that turns from unrighteousness to righteousness determines our spiritual life.

Ephesians 6:15 informs us to have our feet shod. That means to put on shoes or sandals. We are to be prepared or ready to provide the gospel of peace or the good message of the gospel. The gospel is a peace treaty between God and man. It is literally bringing peace, rest, prosperity, quietness in the lives of those who hear and receive it.

In Exodus 12:11, the Israelites were commanded to eat the Passover with their loins girded, shoes on their feet, and staff in their hand. They were to be prepared and ready for the journey. That is how it should be with us, we are to be ready at all times to provide the gospel of peace that is the means of reconciling man to God.

Only God's soldiers have the life raft (the gospel) that can save the multitudes drowning in the sea of sin. The gospel is a lighthouse capable of giving light to those tossed in the sea of sin and guide them to safety.

Ephesians 6:16 tells us the shield of faith is what will prevent evil darts from the enemy penetrating our armor. We are to hold up our shield in front of our coverings or armor. Our shield of faith is held up to protect us from the enemy's fiery darts or weapons.

God's soldiers must comprehend that Satan's darts, his spears, his arrows, his missiles, etc. are inflamed with anger, grief, disease, lust, malice, etc. They are not meant to just injure us, but to destroy us. Satan is not interested in only destroying our faith, he wants to kill us. We stand in his way of propagating his lies, his evil, his anti-God rhetoric, etc.

As we stand in supernatural faith, those *fiery darts* are disabled. They will be quenched. They will be extinguished. Those darts are supernatural, spiritual weapons and the natural man (our flesh) cannot see them nor has any defense against them. If we try to fight in our natural or fleshly man, we will end up like the sons of Sceva in Acts 19:13–16.

Yes, they were not saved, but the point is they were in the flesh. The devil knows if we are dressed in God's armor or not. He knows if we are standing in fear, unbelief, doubt, etc. and not supernatural faith.

Ephesians 6:17 reveals the helmet of salvation that is our defense of the brain. It defends our brain against those thoughts or desires that could influence our thinking. Our thoughts are influenced by ourselves, family, friends, associates, news, the devil, etc. They are the voices constantly trying to influence what we believe or think.

Only the helmet of salvation and the sword of the Spirit which is the word of God can help us to protect our brain from wrong thoughts, false doctrines, wolves in sheep's clothing, self-deception, etc.

The sword is of the Holy Spirit and He always acts in harmony with God's written word. God's word is quick and powerful and sharper than any two-edged sword (Acts 4:12). It is God's living word that reveals the enemy's lies, tricks, snares, etc. When tempted, when in doubt, when fearful, when sick, we need to quote the word which is sharper than any two-edge sword that will cut in pieces, disable, quench, extinguish the fiery darts or snares of the enemy.

When the devil came at Jesus, what did He do? He stood in God's supernatural armor and used his supernatural sword. He used the word to overcome whatever the devil hurled at him. Jesus knew the power of his two-edged sword, and through the word of God, He sent the devil on his way (Matthew 4:1–11).

Ephesians 6:18 is necessary because the warfare we are fighting against the devil is spiritual. We need to see the importance of prayer and supplication. We are to be continuously petitioning God for ourselves and others. Perseverance means we persist and endure with tenacity or a determination without quitting.

We are to be ever watching for any attempt of the enemy to attack God's soldiers. When we perceive a scheme or maneuver, we immediately go into battle through prayer. Prayer is being clothed in supernatural armor and standing in supernatural faith against the forces of Hell that would try to destroy, hinder, or weaken our resolve to continue. Through prayer, we work together with God to gain the victory and disable Satan's fiery darts.

It's essential that we understand the importance of God's supernatural armor. Only it can equip us with all that is needed to stand in supernatural faith against the enemy. We are engaged in a spiritual battle with evil. We must never forget that our warfare is not against forces of this natural or physical realm, but forces in the supernatural or spiritual realm.

Satan will send fiery darts to confront and overcome our faith as long as we're on this earth. As we have physical exams our whole life, we will have spiritual examinations our whole life to check the strength of our faith. Is it malnourished through a lack of food (God's word), or is it healthy and strong through feeding on God's word?

God's soldiers must remember that we do not fight physical or natural opponents, but supernatural, evil, demonic spirits constantly trying to discourage us, to encourage unbelief or doubt, and to destroy our faith.

Without the whole armor of God, we stand defenseless against the fiery darts of the devil. How can natural (flesh and blood) fight supernatural (spirit beings)? We cannot and that's why when we battle in our flesh, we come away like the sons of Sceva. We come away defeated. God's armor is meant to protect not only our spiritual life, but our natural (fleshly body) from supernatural opponents.

The armor of God protects us defensively and offensively. It enables us to have supernatural faith that disables or quenches any fiery dart of unbelief, doubt, sickness, lack, false doctrine, falsehoods, of the devil. Satan has no fiery dart that can penetrate or overcome God's armor when we are fully clothed in it.

Without the armor, we are physically unprotected against lies that claim there is no cure. Because this book is also concerned with God's soldiers overcoming the attacks against our physical body, I will interject a story that I've told before. When I was hospitalized for ulcerative colitis, I was told that I had to live with it. There was no cure. But as the doctor said those words, I heard in my spirit, "That is a lie, I am He that healeth thee." Of course, I thought I would be instantly healed, but I was not. When I sought the Lord,

He told me, "Trust me, I will lead you. Your body was created to heal itself. Follow my instructions, and I will heal you."

More about our body's ability to heal itself will be discussed in chapter eight. An understanding of our body being the temple of the Holy Ghost will enlighten us to this truth.

Let's continue with what the Lord told me about the false report of no healing for colitis. In the meantime, I was put on medication that had many side effects. When I was discharged from the hospital, I was on a strict diet. I stuck with the diet and took the prescriptions prescribed. At the same time, I prayed and asked the Holy Spirit to direct me online for natural cures. It took time for me to comprehend what would work for me, but I was able to quit the prescriptions. I have been eating normal, adhere to the natural supplements, and I am fine. That was over eight years ago.

If I had believed the evil report, I would not have confronted what I was told in the whole armor of God, and stood in supernatural faith that believed God. I withstood the fiery darts daily. Yes, I had the pain, the diarrhea, fatigue, etc. However, supernatural faith told me the physical (what I was seeing) was the lie, the spiritual (what I did not see) had my healing!

Chapter 4

Masters of His Armor

> For though we walk in the flesh, we do not war after the flesh. For the weapons of our warfare are not carnal, but mighty through God to the pulling down of strongholds; Casting down imaginations, and every high thing that exalteth itself against the knowledge of God, and bringing into captivity every thought to the obedience of Christ
> (2 Corinthians 10:3–5).

To be a master of God's armor, we must have a comprehensive knowledge or skill in its use. This will take a great deal of time, effort, and desire on our part. However, once we master our supernatural armor, we become proficient in disabling and quenching the fiery darts of Satan.

Until we comprehend that the word of God is our teacher or instructor in the proficiency of our armor, we will lack in our ability. Why is that so? Since faith comes by hearing and hearing by the word of God (Romans 10:17), our faith is strengthened through believing the word heard. As we hear the word, its truths begin to take root in us. Once truth has a firm hold on what we believe, supernatural faith is enabled to stand against any storm, obstacle, strategy, or fiery dart of the devil.

> And he said to them all, If any man will come after me,
> let him deny himself, and take up his cross daily, and fol-
> low me (Luke 9:23).

Of course, the first place the armor must be effectively used, is to combat our own flesh. Unless we deny, forbid, prevent our flesh what it's feeling, desiring, or wanting, we will NEVER stand in God's supernatural armor that enables supernatural faith to withstand, disable, or quench the fiery darts of Satan. It's imperative to realize that if we cannot use our supernatural armor to combat our own flesh, we will never be able to do spiritual warfare against the evil forces of the devil and triumph over them.

How can we use our supernatural armor to deny and overcome our flesh? We use the breastplate of righteousness to protect our heart against wrong affections. Our loins girt with the truth of the word of God enables us to recognize false doctrines, false preachers, wolves in sheep's clothing, self-deception, etc. The truth enables us to recognize where the enemy lies in wait to deceive us. The shield of faith prevents any fiery darts of the enemy penetrating our armor. The helmet of salvation protects our brain or mind against wrong thoughts, lust of the flesh, lust of the eyes, pride of life, or entertaining the devil's lies. The sword of the Spirit is the word of God that will disable, quench, cut to pieces any fiery dart or snare of the enemy. Prayer is the spiritual weapon that aligns us with God and his strength to strengthen us to withstand against the evil day.

As Gods' soldiers become masters of our supernatural armor, we will confront fleshly appetites and supernatural enemies will become easier to confront. Our fleshly desires, fears, wants, etc. hinder us from confronting the fiery darts. That's why we need to become proficient and skilled in the use of God's supernatural armor and become unskilled and incompetent in our own or natural resources.

We need to stop leaning on our understanding and using carnal or fleshly means against the fiery darts and lean on our supernatural armor. Our flesh and blood armor or our human weapons are powerless against a supernatural enemy. It would be like putting up our hand to stop an atomic missile. Yes, that sounds ridiculous, but that's what many of God's soldiers are doing. We are standing in our flesh or natural man and we are getting clobbered.

It's time to realize that we cannot engage in spiritual warfare in our flesh or our human nature with all its frailties and all its moral weaknesses. Our weapons are not carnal or that which is natural or physical, but supernatural, spiritual, and capable through God.

The verses in 2 Corinthians are military and denote the characteristics of soldiers. All Christians are the soldiers of God Almighty. We must not confront a supernatural and spiritual enemy in the natural or physical. Only God's supernatural weapons can bring down a supernatural enemy.

Only God's weapons cast down man's imaginations, man's reasoning, man's knowledge, and man's understanding. We must comprehend that whatever we see, hear, or read influences our thinking. Our thinking is manipulated, influenced, directed, controlled by whatever is fed into our brain.

We must become masters of our supernatural armor. It's vital to keep our helmet of salvation in place. Our mind is our battlefield or our combat zone. That is where the battle between flesh and Spirit rages. How we think will determine our inner battle of choice. This truth is made clear in my book, *Flesh and Spirit Conflict: The Inner Battle of Choice*.

Wrong thoughts can originate from our own desires, imaginations, and wants. All wrong thoughts will resist, oppose, and set themselves against the knowledge of God. We are not to be a slave or servant to our thinking. Through the truth of God's word, Christ has set us free (John 8:32,36). The grace of God gives us the power to battle our sinful nature as well as the spiritual forces of the devil.

Our supernatural armor enables us to resist anything that is contrary to the truth of God's word. Only the helmet of salvation will keep our mind from being influenced, swayed, or persuaded to believe anything contrary to God's word or God's promises.

Quenching the fiery darts is influenced by what we believe. Do we believe God loves us? Do we genuinely love God? If we can't believe He loves us, we will never believe that our supernatural armor will protect us from the enemy's fiery darts.

We must hold the line at all times and allow no breach of the enemy. God has given us the supernatural armor that enables us to stand against the enemy in supernatural faith. We have the overcoming power. We must not allow the devil to make us think otherwise. He is a liar and will do whatever he can to convince us to run instead of standing. He knows if we are standing in our supernatural armor, we have the supernatural faith to disable and quench all his fiery darts.

Let me refer again to my Christian fiction book, *The Elfdins and the Gold Temple*. In it I revealed what takes place when Christians believe the lies or evil report of the devil. Oralee is a supernatural world that was void of evil until an evil prophet entered by deceitful means. He trained one of the Elfdins in the ways of black powers. This Elfdin convinced the others through deception that they had lost the supernatural powers given to them by the Sovereign God. Now, they had reverted to natural or physical means to combat a supernatural enemy.

That's what Satan tries to do to God's soldiers. He uses lies and deceit to convince us we are powerless against what is occurring. He wants us to believe he has power over us. However, if we are grounded in God's word, we know that Christ has given us power and authority over all the power of the devil (Luke 10:19).

Satan works overtime to convince us that God's word is not true. He used that evil report on Eve in the Garden of Eden (Genesis 3:1). Once the devil influences us to doubt or question the validity, the integrity, the verity of God's word, we go from supernatural faith to unbelief.

Without God's soldiers being clothed in the supernatural armor of God, everything that is seen, heard, or read will enter into our hearts unfiltered. All that is impure or contrary to God and his word will become part of our affections or what we believe.

Only as we learn to master our supernatural armor are we enabled to take every thought, our thinking, our logic, our reasoning and filter them to make them obedient to Christ. Our supernatural armor empowers us to cast down or bring to nought all influences to our thinking that are opposite, against, or contrary to God's word.

As I stated in *Faith's Journey Confronts Obstacles*, the Lord, many years ago, gave me a vision concerning our supernatural armor. It was during a time when I was doing a week-long revival. Before that particular night, I was praying about the lack of overcoming in God's soldiers.

What the Lord disclosed to me was like the War of Independence. I watched as soldiers came back on stretchers, carts full of soldiers with legs missing, arms severed, heads wrapped, eye patches. All were wounded and bloodied.

My mind was confused, and I asked the Lord what it was all about. He then took me to another place where they had come from before going to battle. What I saw before me were piles of shoes, helmets, breastplates, shields, girdles, and swords. God said to me, "My people insist on going against the enemy without my full armor and they are wounded, discouraged, and even destroyed. I have supplied the armor, but they are not using it. Then they accuse me of not helping, not protecting, not loving, and forsaking them."

We are to put on our supernatural armor. That is our responsibility. God has provided it, but we are to clothe ourselves in it. It's time to reconsider how we go to battle. If we have not learned how to use our armor, we need to start immediately. As we decipher how each piece works, we begin to understand its necessity. As we grow in knowledge and understanding of God's word, we have the wherewith to answer him that reproaches us (Psalms 119:42).

The supernatural armor of God is our defense against all the influences that affect our thoughts or that which we meditate upon. Whatever influences our thought process, if not filtered through the armor, is Satan's stronghold. If we believe evil reports, we continuously try to do warfare in our flesh.

Our faith is unprotected without the armor of God. There is no faith in the natural realm that can overcome a supernatural enemy. Our fleshly, carnal, natural weapons are of this realm and we need to rise up into the supernatural realm to fight an invisible enemy. If we don't learn to master our armor, we will come back from battle like the soldiers in my vision. God has given us all we need to confront our flesh and the fiery darts of the enemy. Masters of God's supernatural armor live and stand in supernatural faith that disables and quenches all the fiery darts (lies, evil reports, doubt, fear, sickness, etc.) of the wicked!

Chapter 5

Healing Is the Children's Bread

Then Jesus went thence, and departed into the coasts of Tyre and Sidon. And behold, a woman of Canaan came out of the same coasts and cried unto him, saying, Have mercy on me, O Lord, thou son of David; my daughter is grievously vexed with a devil. But he answered her not a word. And his disciples came and besought him, saying, Send her away; for she crieth after us. But he answered and said, I am not sent but unto the lost sheep of the house of Israel. Then came she and worshipped him, saying, Lord, help me. But he answered and said, It is not meet to take the children's bread and to cast it to dogs. And she said, Truth, Lord; yet the dogs eat of the crumbs which fall from their masters' table. Then Jesus answered and said unto her, O woman, great is thy faith: be it unto thee even as thou wilt. And her daughter was made whole from that very hour (Matthew 15:21–28).

In these scripture verses, we have a gentile or Palestinian woman seeking the Lord for the healing of her demon vexed daughter.

As we read the dialect or conversation between Jesus and the gentile woman, we comprehend Jesus was emphatic that what she was seeking belonged to the children of God. He clearly informed her that it was not meet—it was not right or proper—to take the children's bread and give it to dogs (the Jewish term referring to gentiles).

I sense to put a story in here. A man we knew left the Lord because he claimed God is prejudice by calling women dogs. We tried to explain to him that it was the Jewish term for gentiles whether men or women. Anyway, he wanted nothing to do with a God who discriminated against women.

If we have an improper understanding about God through a lack of biblical knowledge, we will NEVER walk in supernatural faith that overcomes. When Jesus used the word *dog*, He was merely using the common speech to express that gentiles were outside the covenant rights of Israel.

The bread of healing was for the children only. The Greek word implies *shew* bread. And we are aware that the shewbread belonged to the priests only. Here it implies the bread belonged to the children only.

Let's start to understand the bread by clarifying its meaning or significance.

> Give us this day our daily bread (Matthew 6:11).

Daily bread in the Greek means for subsistence. It is needful daily. Our daily bread or loaf is necessary for survival.

Subsistence is defined as to live, to be maintained with food and clothing. Competent provisions, the means of supporting life. That which supplies the means of living, as money, pay, or wages.

As we look at that definition, it covers spiritual, physical, and material. Competent provisions of supporting life can be spiritual or physical. But food, clothing, and money are physical and material. Thus, our daily bread includes all that is needed whether spiritual, physical, or material.

Let's go back to the text in Matthew 15. When Jesus referred to the children's bread, He meant that the Jews were the first children of the kingdom. The bread referred to the benefits that Christ (the Messiah) would bring to the children.

These benefits include salvation for the spirit, soul, and body of man. That means deliverance from sin, sickness, disease, poverty, demons, satanic power, the flesh, etc. Simply put, salvation means deliverance. It is deliverance from all that is NOT good or beneficial to spirit, soul, or body. Christ on Calvary delivered us from all that is contrary to the abundant life in him (John 10:10).

God's soldiers must understand this daily bread. We must comprehend the benefits of salvation for spirit, soul, and body are *family rights, legal rights, promised rights, redemptive rights*. These rights belong to ALL the children of God.

Jesus made it unequivocally clear to the gentile woman that she did not possess any family or legal rights to the benefits belonging to the children. Not just healing, but all that is included in the daily bread promised to his children.

Yet, this woman is incredible. By stating, *yet the dogs eat of the crumbs which fall from their master's table*, she is acknowledging she is a gentile with no family rights. She acknowledges the dogs may not sit at the table and eat with the children, but they do receive the crumbs.

As the dogs have the right to claim the crumbs, she was doing likewise. This is what she is saying in verse twenty-seven, "I don't desire to take the loaf provided for the favored children, but only the crumbs they leave." She was claiming the rights of the dogs to receive the crumbs or scraps that would be thrown away.

Wow! What Faith! This woman believed the crumbs were enough to heal her daughter. She knew the benefits for the children were of such value that crumbs were sufficient or enough to supply her daughter's need for healing. Her faith is astounding, and Jesus marveled at such faith.

> But without faith it is impossible to please him; for he that cometh to God must believe that he is and that he is a rewarder of them that diligently seek him (Hebrews 11:6).

Let's understand what this verse is communicating to us. It is saying that God is delighted or pleased when we come to him and believe that He is and that He is a rewarder, reciprocator, or compensator. We are being told that God wants us to expect reward, our prayer answered, or his promise fulfilled.

This gentile woman not only believed who He is, but expected him to reward her. She expected him to heal her daughter.

God wants to reward or recompense us. But He can only do it when we believe. He only recompenses faith. We must believe him to do it. Thus, when faith comes to God, it receives.

> Ask, and it shall be given you; seek and ye shall find; knock and it shall be opened unto you. For everyone that asketh receiveth; and he that seeketh findeth; and to him that knocketh it shall be opened (Matthew 7:7–8).

This asking, seeking, and knocking is done according to Hebrews 11:6. We must understand this fact. Only when faith asks, it receives. Only when faith seeks, it finds. Only when faith knocks, the door is opened. Whatever is not of faith will not please God and will not receive from him.

> And this is the confidence that we have in him, that, if we ask any thing according to his will, he heareth us: And if we know that he hear us, whatsoever we ask, we know that we have the petitions that we desired of him (1 John 5:14–15).

Now, I'll give a hard truth. Just because we ask, seek, or knock does not mean it is God's will. How many times do we ask for what we desire or want? How many times do we pray for something opposite of his word?

If we ask, seek, or knock and don't receive, it's not that God is not willing to reward. It's either that it wasn't God's will or we waivered, doubted, staggered in our faith (James 1:6).

Let me give an example of it not being in God's will. It's a simple illustration, but it's usually more easily understood. We pray and ask God to bless this chocolate cake to our body. Yet, we have severe diabetes and know we are not to eat it. It is not a prayer of faith, but it is tempting God. Our prayer will not be answered. We knew we should practice self-denial and didn't.

It's like jumping out of an airplane without a parachute and asking him for a safe landing. That sounds ridiculous, but how many do that daily in our prayer requests? How many of us insist on asking what goes against God's word?

There should be no question about God rewarding healing for our faith to believe him. Jesus himself said that healing is the children's bread. Our whole spirit, soul, and body were healed on Calvary (Isaiah 53:5; 1 Peter 2:24). However, I mentioned in the *Introduction* that the only time we may have to endure sickness and disease is if we have received a thorn in the flesh. With the thorn will come sufficient grace to withstand the thorn (2 Corinthians 12:7–9). For more clarity on that subject, please refer to my book, *Satan's Strategy to Torment Through Physical Ambush*.

Okay, let's get back to the gentile woman. She knew Jesus could heal her daughter. She believed scraps or crumbs, that which the children consider garbage, was valuable enough to supply her need.

She saw the value in the mere scraps of the children. She saw the children's daily bread so valuable that even the crumbs of the loaf were sufficient to heal her daughter.

We, the children of God, the children of faith, receive the whole loaf. The whole loaf is ours. Yet, the children are, for the most part, in need and lacking because of doubt, wavering, and unbelief. How many sit as Job scraping their sores instead of believing healing is our bread? How many pray for healing and waver when it doesn't happen instantly? Why do we forget that faith is the substance of what we hope for, yet is unseen in the physical?

We need to grasp hold of the truth that our daily bread is every promise, blessing, benefit of God's word. Every promise of God written in his word belongs to his children. Each promise is our legal right, our family right as his child.

With that understanding, we know that healing IS the children's bread. We know it is our family right, our legal right. Because God promises it, we expect healing. Thus, as we stand in God's supernatural armor enabling supernatural faith, God rewards or recompenses our faith with the healing!

Chapter 6

God Is Our Physician

And said, If thou wilt diligently hearken to the voice of
the Lord thy God, and wilt do that which is right in his
sight, and wilt give ear to his commandments, and keep
all his statutes, I will put none of these diseases upon
thee, which I have brought upon the Egyptians: for I
am the Lord that healeth thee (Exodus 15:26).

THE SCRIPTURE TEXT IN Exodus, informs us that if we earnestly
heed and follow God's word, he will keep the diseases brought upon
the Egyptians from us.

Then He reveals the most important fact in the verse: *I am the
Lord that healeth thee.* The Hebrew word for *Lord* and *healeth* gives
us *Jehovah Rapha* which means the Lord that heals, cures, repairs,
mends, makes whole.

However, the word *Rapha* also means physician. That means
that God is the self-existent, eternal physician or healer.

Now, knowing that God is *Physician* is useless. I mean, unless
we understand that He is MY personal physician.

In order to understand this truth, we must separate the spiritual from the physical in order for faith to work. To do this, we must

think differently. We have to be transformed by the renewing of our mind (Romans 12:2).

In simple terms, we have to think like God which comes as we know the word. Let me explain what I mean using the following scripture verse.

> Be not deceived; God is not mocked; for whatsoever a man soweth, that shall he also reap (Galatians 6:7).

The word of God is like seed planted. Whatever we plant is what we will harvest. We reap what we sow. Our crop harvested is determined by the seed we planted.

Now, if God is my physician, then He is my healer. We must comprehend this truth. We must KNOW that it's God's will to heal us. Unless, that is settled in our minds and spirit, we cannot approach healing without being double minded and wavering.

> But let him ask in faith, nothing wavering. For he that wavereth is like a wave of the sea driven with the wind and tossed. For let not that man think that he shall receive anything of the Lord (James 1:6–7).

Believing in healing is not enough. Let me explain. It's like saying, "I believe in healing. I know God could heal me right now IF He wanted to. That's like saying, "I know God could save me right now IF He wanted to.

There are NO if's with God.

> For all the promises of God in him are yea, and in him Amen, unto the glory of God by us (2 Corinthians 1:20).

This tells us clearly that not one promise in God's word is *NO* to any who will believe and meet his conditions. The scripture text in Exodus 15:26 verifies that when we meet God's requirements, He will heal us. There is no IF He will heal. He promises when we do what is right in his sight and obey his word, He WILL heal us.

When we were born again, we believed the word we heard, faith birthed in us and we were transformed from spiritual death to spiritual life. (This is explained in more detail in my book, *Faith's Journey Confronts Obstacles*).

It was an incredible transformation. What we must comprehend is that faith comes for healing the same way it came for salvation.

> So then faith comes by hearing, and hearing by the Word of God (Romans 10:17).

As we hear the word, we continue to develop (build-up, strengthen) our faith to receive our healing. When the word strengthens our faith, the force of that faith then rises up in us to receive God's healing power in our body. This same process took place when we became born again. We must understand that only faith pleases God and only faith receives from God.

> But without faith it is impossible to please him: for he that cometh to God must believe that he is, and that he is a rewarder of them that diligently seek him (Hebrews 11:6).

The word planted in our heart convinced us that God is and that He would save us. Now, we must plant the word in our heart until we believe God is our physician and when faith's power rises in us, we are healed (1 Peter 2:24, Isaiah 53:5).

> My son, attend to my words; incline thine ear unto my sayings. Let them not depart from thine eyes; keep them in the midst of thine heart. For they are life unto those that find them, and health to all their flesh (Proverbs 4:20–22).

The scriptures in Proverbs are similar to the verses in Exodus. But we have to look carefully at some words in Proverbs.

First of all, *attend to my words* means pay attention to them. He's telling us to turn attention towards them. *Let them not depart from thine eyes* means don't go away from them. We must not turn aside from his words.

Keep them in the midst of thine heart means to hold onto them as a prized possession. Retain them in our mind or in our understanding.

IF we continue in the word, we are promised eternal life and health to our flesh. These verses prove physical healing is also part of Christ's atonement of redemptive work on the cross.

Why do I claim that? Health to our flesh is PHYSICAL health. Our flesh is not spiritual health, but physical health.

> Beloved, I wish above all else that thou mayest prosper and be health, even as thy soul prospereth (3 John 2).

The word health in that verse means to have sound health; to be well in body. That is our physical body that is to be in health.

> When the even was come, they brought unto him many that were possessed with devils: and he cast out the spirits with his word, and healed all that were sick; That it might be fulfilled which was spoken by Esaias the prophet, saying, Himself took our infirmities, and bare our sicknesses (Matthew 8:16–17).

On the cross of Calvary, Jesus's atoning death redeemed (delivered, emancipated, rescued, liberated) the whole person—spirit, soul, and physical body.

Sin and sickness are Satan's design or his means to destroy us. Forgiveness and healing are God's design or his means to redeem us and make us whole.

Only when we awaken to our full rights in the Word of God will we realize that health of body as well as health of soul belongs to us.

Jesus died to give it to us. We accept salvation (deliverance) of the soul (our spiritual body) when we are born again, But we must comprehend that it also includes salvation (deliverance) of our flesh (our physical body).

To help us understand the meaning of salvation more clearly, we will look at the Hebrew for salvation. It translates from various words such as deliverance, victory, prosperity, health, welfare, preserve, liberty, and safety. Then in the Greek, it means rescue or safety (physically or morally) deliver, health.

The point is that Christ's atoning work on the cross included physical health as well as spiritual health. We must comprehend that truth in order for faith to believe its physician.

We go to human doctors who are part of the natural realm and we listen to them. We take their prescribed medications. In other words, we put our trust or faith in them. But what are they?

They are men. Mankind with all its flaws, its inabilities, its limited knowledge, and its variables. Yet, God is perfect. He is omnipotent (able to do anything). He is omniscient (knows everything about everything). He is immutable (can never change or waiver). God has the faith that speaks what does not exist into existence.

Let's continue with believing our physician.

> But he was wounded for our transgressions, he was bruised
> for our iniquities: the chastisement of our peace was upon
> him; and with his stripes we are healed (Isaiah 53:5).

The word healed is *Rapha*. Again, it means spiritual healing and physical healing. It means to mend, to cure, to heal, to repair, to make whole.

In Proverbs 4:22, we are told that God's word is health to our whole physical body (all their flesh). This is an important fact if we are to walk in supernatural faith.

Remember I said the word of God is like seed planted? It was God's word planted in our hearts that enabled faith to birth and bring forth salvation. Faith rose up in us and brought forth the harvest of salvation. We became born again.

Now, although we believe in healing, we must plant the seed (the word of God) in our hearts. Without the healing seed from God's word planted in our heart, we have nothing in the ground to produce a harvest.

If a farmer plants no seed, he will produce no crop. There will be no harvest of a good crop. All he will produce is weeds that are useless.

As we plant healing scriptures, our faith is strengthened. We understand our physician is God who can do anything. He can do the impossible. What He promised in his word He will and can do. He will never change.

It's faith in our physician's ability, his knowledge, his medicine (his word), etc. that brings forth our healing. We believe our physician to perform what He promised. We have confidence in his faith to do it. It's not confidence in our faith or our ability, but an assurance in his supernatural faith to bring about his promise.

He has the faith to heal us. We don't do the healing, He does. For illumination about God's faith, see my book, *Satan Has No Authority Over God's Soldier: Illuminating Godlike Faith.*

We didn't have to save ourselves, He did it.

We know He created all things through his faith. We don't have the faith to create all things, but He does. Supernatural armor enables supernatural faith that believes in God's supernatural power and ability.

As the force of faith comes out of our heart, the seed or the word of God that spoke all things into existence brings forth the harvest. We can't earn salvation or any of God's promises or blessings.

> For by grace are ye saved through faith; and that not of yourselves: it is the gift of God: Not of works, lest any man should boast (Ephesians 2:8–9).

Everything God does is the benefit of his grace. We deserve no blessing. We can earn no promise. Our sins deserve and have earned Hell. But God's grace has offered us forgiveness and blessings through the means of faith at the conference table.

Now, it's through faith that we are saved. It's through faith that we are healed. God's grace saves, heals, etc. when we believe his word and receive what He promises.

God wants us to be healthy. Sin and sickness are part of the Fall. In Christ, forgiveness and health are part of the atonement. Christ's sacrificial death redeemed the whole man. That means spirit, soul, and body. He delivered us from the curse of sin, and all it entailed.

As faith birthed for salvation, we must let that same supernatural faith rise in us for healing. Unbelief will not receive forgiveness, and it will not receive healing.

The word planted revealed to our heart who God is and that He promises forgiveness for our sins. Upon faith rising in us, we accepted the forgiveness and became born again.

Now, as the word planted reveals to our heart who God is and that He promises healing to our flesh (our whole physical being) faith rises and causes us to accept healing in our body.

Let me explain something to help us comprehend. As God (Christ) is our personal savior, He is our personal physician.

We must say, "As Jesus is my personal savior, He is my personal physician. As Jesus is my personal savior, He is my personal Physician," until faith rises in us and God can perform the healing.

Now, let me give some facts, some unchangeable truths about our personal physician.

1. Faith's physician resides in the spiritual (supernatural) realm that is far superior to the physical (natural) realm.
2. Faith's physician possesses supernatural ability and not natural ability.
3. Faith's physician is infinite (without limit) and not finite (limited) like man.
4. Faith's physician possesses perfect faith that speaks worlds into existence.
5. Faith's physician is the personal physician, doctor, healer to all who are the children of faith.
6. Faith's physician is the Lord God Almighty.

Understanding God is the physician of his children enables us to comprehend that faith generates from the supernatural realm. We don't look at what we see or feel, because we believe we have what our physician promised (Hebrews 11:1). Standing on the truth that healing is the children's bread, God's supernatural armor creates supernatural faith that disables or quenches the fiery darts of sickness and disease. Supernatural faith believes its supernatural physician is our healer!

Chapter 7

God's Word Is Faith's Medicine

> Bless the Lord, O my soul, and forget not all his benefits:
> Who forgiveth all thine iniquities; who healeth all thy
> diseases (Psalm 103:2–3).
> Who his own self bare our sins in his own body on the
> tree, that we, being dead to sins, should live unto righ-
> teousness: by whose stripes ye were healed (1 Peter 2:24).

First and foremost, we must know that it is God's will to heal us. Unless that is settled in our minds and spirit, we cannot approach healing without being double minded and wavering.

> But let him ask in faith, nothing wavering. For he that
> wavereth is like a wave of the sea driven with the wind
> and tossed. For let not that man think that he shall re-
> ceive any thing of the Lord (James 1:6–7).

Believing in healing is not enough. I can say I believe this chair will hold me up, but never sit in it. We can say we believe, but believe is an action word. Faith is not passive. It is active and dynamic.

> Thou believest that there is one God; thou doest well: the
> devils also believe and tremble (James 2:19).

We must act on that belief through faith. We must know that it's God's will for us to be healed.

The seed we plant is the word. Faith gets its nutriment from the word. The word of God is the incorruptible seed. It cannot be spoiled, become rotten, or be weakened by any disease or any other force Satan has to offer. Wherever the word is planted, it will produce. However, the ground in which it is sown determines the degree of harvest.

> The sower soweth the word. And these are they by the way side, where the word is sown; but when they have heard, Satan cometh immediately, and taketh away the word that was sown in their hearts. And these are they likewise which are sown on stony ground; who, when they have heard the word, immediately receive it with gladness; And have no root in themselves, and so endure but for a time: afterward, when affliction or persecution ariseth for the word's sake, immediately they are offended. And these are they which are sown among thorns; such as hear the word, And the cares of this world, and the deceitfulness of riches, and the lusts of other things entering in, choke the word, and it becometh unfruitful. And these are they which are sown on good ground; such as hear the word, and receive it, and bring forth fruit, some thirtyfold, some sixty, and some an hundred (Mark 4:14–20).

The first seed sown is by the wayside. Here Satan comes immediately and takes away the word that was sown in our hearts. Whether of doubt, unbelief, or tradition is not important. The point is that the sown seed was snatched by Satan before it could bring forth a harvest.

The second seed sown is on stony ground. It has no root in itself. As soon as we are tested because of the word, we become offended. The point again is that it was sown and received. But before it could take root, we did not stand or have confidence in the word when tested. Whenever we receive revelational knowledge, we will be tested to stand on that word.

The third seed sown is among the thorns. The cares of this world, the deceitfulness of riches, and the lusts of other things in our heart will choke the word so that it cannot become fruitful. The point here is that we have our hearts (our thoughts, our life, and our energy) set on the cares of this world.

The fourth seed sown is on good ground. Seed sown here brings forth fruit some thirty-fold, some sixty, and some an hundred. The point here is that the word sown is free from hindrances, the crop produced will be God's will for our life.

Our heart is the ground where the seed is sown. Once we're born again, our heart is capable of being good ground. What we must comprehend is that when we became born again, the same supernatural faith with which God created the worlds through was born into us. Of course not at the degree as that of God, but it is still supernatural faith capable of moving mountains (Matthew 17:20).

> So then faith comes by hearing, and hearing by the word of God (Romans 10:17).

Faith comes for healing the same way it came for salvation. As we heard the word concerning salvation, it became fruitful and produced salvation. As we hear the word concerning healing, it becomes fruitful and produces healing.

As we hear the word, we continue to develop (build-up) our faith to receive our healing. Why? Because the force of that faith rises up in our heart to receive God's healing power in our body as it did for salvation.

We must plant the seed. Even if we believe in healing, without the healing seed from God's Word planted in our hearts, we have nothing in the ground to produce a harvest.

If we don't plant seed, we will not produce a crop. No crop means there will be nothing to harvest. We cannot expect to harvest what we don't plant. We reap what we sow (Galatians 6:7). No seed means no crop.

Faith receives its nutriment from the word of God. The more word (nourishment or food) the stronger our faith. Whatever our faith is lacking, the word or medicine needed will strengthen and heal our faith.

Don't get me wrong, we don't need more faith. We've all received the measure of faith (Romans 12:3).

> And the apostles said unto the Lord, Increase our faith. And the Lord said, If ye had faith as a grain of mustard seed, ye might say unto this sycamine tree, Be thou plucked up by the root, and be thou planted in the sea; and it should obey you (Luke 17:5–6).

Again, we see that it's not the size, amount, or extent of faith, but the strength of our faith that determines what is accomplished. Faith the size of a grain of mustard seed can be sufficiently strengthened to have a sycamine tree plucked up by the root and planted in the sea.

Now, as the force of faith comes out of our heart, the seed (word of God) sown or planted brings forth fruit. First it brings forth salvation. Second it brings forth obedience. Third it brings forth the fruit of the Spirit. Fourth it will bring forth healing, prosperity, etc. It will bring forth whatever God has promised.

If fruit is to be produced, we must give our undivided attention to the word of God and take heed to what it says. We must be doers of the word and not hearers only.

When we became born again, we paid attention to God's word. We heeded or did what it said. We believed that God was able to save us, and we believed He would if we asked him. However, we must believe, we must know it is God's will to heal us, as we knew it was his will to save us.

Man's knowledge, science, medicine will not strengthen our faith. It would be like drinking Kool-Aid and believing it is medicine. If man's knowledge or power is our foundation upon which we build faith, our faith (spiritual, supernatural faith) will be deficient.

Let me explain this further. We have a car that needs to have high octane gas to run properly, but we put the wrong fuel in it. Our car will run sluggish and probably sputter, stall, etc. Now, if it's out of fuel, and we don't put any in, it will not run at all.

Our faith is like that car, it can only be as active as the fuel supply. Now, if we take in the wrong fuel (wrong doctrine, false teachings, unbelief), our faith will be sluggish. If we don't put any fuel in at all, our faith will die.

Sickness and disease in our body are like bad fuel in a car. As the car is sluggish, etc. so is our body. Sickness, disease, etc. make our body deficient, sluggish, etc. And a lack of the word of God (God's medicine) makes our body unable to run normal.

Faith can only be as strong or as healthy as the medicine it is given. Our faith gets its strength, its nutriments from the word of God. We need our spiritual medicine, vitamins, nutriments found in the word to have a strong and healthy faith.

Faith's medicine is the word of God. The word of God is our physician's medicine. Yet it is not applied to the sickness, disease, pain, etc. in our body. That may sound confusing, but it is the revelation needed to be healed.

Faith's physician is God. The omnipotent (the all-powerful Spirit being); the omnipresent (the everywhere present Spirit being); the omniscient (the all-knowing Spirit being); the immutable (the never changing Spirit being).

God is love. God is Healer. God is grace. God is faith. God is the author and originator of faith. God's faith spoke all things that exist into existence. Nothing existed until God said, "Let there be."

> He sent his word, and healed them, and delivered them
> (Psalm 107:20).

The word sent in the Hebrew is translated as spread or sow. Now, we know the word of God is the seed sown. Christ made that clear in Matthew 13:9. Because the word sown was not understood, they did not have the faith necessary to bring forth fruit.

Hebrews 11:6 says that only faith is acceptable or pleasing to God. He will not accept anything less. No sacrifice, offering, etc. Only faith is acceptable.

It is not quoting the word of God that saves us any more than quoting it will heal us. Yes, the word of God is faith's medicine. But it is not the word that saves or heals us.

Faith's physician is not the word, it is God. It is God who saves, heals, and blesses us. Our faith must be in our physician. Faith must be in his faith, his ability, his power, etc.

Without faith, without believing that God will do what He promises, there is no salvation, no answered prayer, no fulfilled promises, and there is no physical healing. The devils believe and tremble (James 2:19), but they will not be saved or healed.

Let me repeat that the word does not heal us any more than it saved us. It is faith in the word of God. It's faith in God's love, in God's promises, in God's ability, in God's FAITH.

It's knowing that if God said it, He is not only able to perform it, but has the faith to bring it to pass.

Faith cannot be conjured up like pumping a tire or something. But as we hear the word of God, read the word of God, and understand, comprehend, grasp, absorb it, our faith is strengthened.

The deeper in we go into the word, the weightier it becomes. As a body builder is built up by lifting heavier weights, our faith is built up or strengthened by a deeper knowledge of God's word.

The word is the fuel our faith runs on. God's word is the only medicine, the only remedy, the only prescription that strengthens faith. God only accepts faith.

Faith is a spiritual quality. It is not found in the natural or physical realm. Thus, only spiritual fuel or medicine will enable it to work.

Heal me, O Lord, and I shall be healed (Jeremiah 17:14).

Man's knowledge, science, medicine, wisdom, etc. are part of the natural or physical realm. They will not and cannot produce faith in God. We may read scientific journals about health, but they will never produce the medicine necessary to bring forth supernatural faith that disables or quenches whatever fiery dart or strategy the devil hurls at us.

God gave us his word through the power of the Holy Spirit so that we may have access to it. For without it, we could never have the faith that He accepts. We would not know him. Why? Because it's the word of God that reveals or testifies of him (John 5:39).

Without understanding, without believing the word of God, there would be no salvation, no healing, no blessings.

The medicine of faith is God's word. Through the medicine of God's word, if we have weak faith, it is the booster shot needed to strengthen it. When our faith is strengthened, we believe in God's ability to perform his promises. We understand that God cannot change. God will never change his promises, his ability, etc. He has faith in his power. He knows He is not lacking anything to accomplish his promise. God has no unbelief. He is incapable of unbelief. Faith is one of his attributes. Faith is part of who and what God is.

Once we comprehend the necessity for our faith's medicine, we will devour the word of God. As we take in the nutriments needed, we will stand clothed in God's supernatural armor and bring forth the supernatural faith of God that disables all fiery darts of sickness, disease, etc.!

Chapter 8

We Are God's Temple

What? know ye not that your body is the temple of the
Holy Ghost which is in you, which ye have of God, and
ye are not your own? For ye are bought with a price:
therefore glorify God in your body, and in your spirit,
which are God's (1 Corinthians 6:19-20).

THIS CHAPTER'S INTENTENTION IS to illuminate why so many are
not overcoming sickness and disease. Unless we comprehend what
it means to be the temple of the Holy Ghost, we will never realize
the potential for healing in our body.

Please understand that this chapter is not denying instanta-
neous healing by the Lord. It is meant to awaken God's children to
the ability of our body to heal itself when properly taken care of. It
also focuses on the results of an improper diet on our body.

Yes, God is our physician and his word is faith's medicine.
There is no question concerning those truths. The problem is that
we expect God to do something when we have not adhered to his
law of reciprocity. In other words, God promises to do something
"IF" we do what He asks us to do. If we don't do it, God will not do
what He promised.

In Leviticus, the laws of health clearly illustrate that God's healing us is not to be considered as an unconditional blessing. As we must walk in fellowship and obedience to God, we are to conform to the precepts that regulate healthful habits and diets which are of his creational design. Proper diet, adequate sleep, exercise, and cleanliness are as much a part of the biblical doctrine of Divine Healing as is anointing and prayer. Furthermore, in Exodus 15:26, God promised to keep all the diseases of the Egyptians from his children IF we diligently hearken to the voice of the Lord, do that which is right in his sight, give ear to his commandments, and keep all his statutes. If we *don't* hearken unto his voice, He will not keep sickness and disease from us.

Now, we find in our scripture text in 1 Corinthians that we are the temple of the Holy Ghost, we were bought with a price, we are to glorify God in our body and spirit, and that we don't belong to self but to God. Unless we comprehend that we are God's property or possession, we will continue to act like we belong to self.

In chapter three, I mentioned my hospitalization with ulcerative colitis. When the doctor told me that I had to live with it, I was stunned. Let me explain more of this story. I had been suffering with it for a couple of years to the point I was vomiting often. I learned the vomiting was due to a dangerously low potassium level. Plus, I had kidney stones and diverticulosis. Anyway, I was quite ill but had no medical insurance or financial means to go to the doctor. When I turned sixty-five, I qualified for Medicare.

It took my being admitted through the emergency room at the hospital to educate me about my body and what God had intended for us. I pray what I learned will help others to comprehend that God DID create our bodies to heal itself.

I have discovered that it is through events in our life that we come away with valuable lessons learned. Through my circumstance, I now comprehend why so many of God's soldiers are unhealthy and why so many are not receiving healing.

> And he said to them all, If any man will come after me, let him deny himself, and take up his cross daily, and follow me (Luke 9:23).

Do Christians truly comprehend what it means to follow Jesus? Do we truly comprehend what deny self means? Do we truly comprehend what it means to take up our cross daily? It seems that we quote the word, but miss the mark in living it. What do I mean by that? We don't comprehend what denying self really is.

In my book, *Flesh and Spirit Conflict: The Inner Battle of Choice*, I mentioned how we think suffering or denying self is having no sugar for our tea or coffee. How many of us misunderstand our self-centeredness for suffering? When we want something but can't have it, we think that is suffering. When in reality, it is a lack of self-denial. Without a comprehension of self-denial according to God, we will never be able to follow him into living a healthy life.

Let me begin to help us understand. If we plant a garden, but we don't take proper care of it, what happens? Our fruit will be eaten by insects and rodents. Our fruit will be overtaken by weeds. Out fruit will wither. It will not be a healthy harvest of ripe and nutritious fruit.

Now, our body is a garden. What are we feeding it? What are we doing to care for it? Do we realize that our body is NOT our own? Do we realize that it has been bought with the blood of Jesus? Do we realize that if we are Christians our body belongs to God? Do we realize that we are *caretakers or custodians* of God's property?

> If any man defile the temple of God, him shall God destroy; for the temple of God is holy, which temple ye are (1 Corinthians 3:17).

Let me clarify what this verse means. If we defile, contaminate, pollute our body, God *will allow* its destruction. We cannot expect to pray for healing when we have not respected our body. We have not treated it like the temple of God. We have not taking care of it. We have neglected it. We have abused it. We have indulged in what has harmed it.

We need to understand it is an intricate machine that needs proper care. We realize that we must take care of our motor vehicle. We put the proper gasoline in it. We make sure the fluids are up to par. We keep good tires on it. We are aware of what is necessary to keep it running properly. Yet, when it comes to God's temple, how many times do we neglect proper care? How many times do we indulge in fast food, junk food, etc. and not eat a nutritious and healthy meal?

Okay, let's proceed in understanding what Christians seem to be missing. It took me being hospitalized for me to become educated. The Lord revealed that He allowed me to become that ill so I could understand that He created our body to heal itself and be enabled to inform others.

The problem is not with our body's ability, but it is with our lack of denying self. Most of us do not deny, forbid, refuse, decline self what it desires. Listen to me, I am not talking about what we know to be sin. I'm talking about over-indulgence in what we eat and drink. I'm talking about eating improperly. This is a diet of malnutrition such as too much or an overindulgence in fatty and greasy food, sweet foods, highly flavored food, too pungent food, processed meats, caffeine, fast foods.

How many eat junk food daily? I mean like salted snack foods, gum, candy, sweet desserts, fried fast food, sugary carbonated beverages. Even hamburgers, pizza, tacos, etc. can be considered junk food depending on their ingredients and preparation methods.

Just because we ask God to bless what we are about to eat doesn't mean it is blessed. He will not bless what we know is not good for our body. If we are a diabetic, God will not bless that chocolate cake. He expects us to deny self what is not good for his temple. That would be like asking the Lord to bless the nicotine to our body. We know nicotine is a dangerous and highly addictive chemical that can cause cancer, an increase in blood pressure, heart rate, flow of blood to the heart and a narrowing of arteries. It can also contribute to the hardening of the arterial walls and lead to a heart attack.

Okay, most of us know about the dangers of nicotine and avoid it. But how many of us know that fast foods or junk food is linked to a higher risk of obesity, depression, digestive issues, heart disease and stroke, high blood pressure, type 2 diabetes, cancer, and early death? Furthermore, fast food is high in sodium, saturated fat, trans fat, and cholesterol.

Why are God's soldiers indulging in what is NOT beneficial or healthy for our bodies? It's quite simple, it's easier to go out to eat rather than cook healthy meals at home. It's easier after a hard day's work to order something. It's easier to grab something at a fast food place rather than pack a healthy lunch. It's tastier to drink some sort of sweet drink instead of drinking water.

Before I continue in that direction, I felt it necessary to point out what may not be known. First of all, I am not saying to avoid doctors. What I am saying is that most doctors will prescribe medications that have adverse effects. They will *not* lead us to what will naturally cure our bodies. They are not trained in natural cures. All they know is the science of the medicine, but not the knowledge of how to help us heal out bodies naturally. So, we are kept ignorant, continue buying our prescriptions to cover our symptoms, are getting more unhealthy, and have no means of being healed.

Let me interject something here. When I asked the doctor about the prescriptions he prescribed, I asked if they would eventually heal. He said they would not. As a matter of fact, I would have to be tested regularly because of the adverse reactions the medicines would cause. I don't fault him, he was going by what he had been educated in. I thank the Lord that it opened my understanding to the ability of my body when properly cared for.

What we neglect to realize is that in the days of Jesus and Paul the Apostle, doctors were more like herbalists. For instance, medicine that would have been used would have been herbs such as *flax* that is used for arthritis, bronchitis, cancer, dermatitis, heart disease, inflammation, rheumatism, etc. *Frankincense* (Boswellia sacra) is used for dysentery, fever, polyps, etc. *Garlic* is used for angina, cancer, colds, diabetes, flu, hypertension, infections, etc. *Milk Thistle* (Silybum marianum) is used for asthma, cirrhosis, hepatitis, jaundice, kidney and urinary tract stones, psoriasis, etc. *Turmeric* (Curcuma longa) is used for inflammation, flatulence, arthritis, bronchitis, diuretic, dyspepsia, expectorant, laryngitis, lymphoma, rheumatism, etc. *Myrrh* (Commiphora spp) is used for analgesic, astringent, bronchitis, expectorant, high cholesterol, etc.

It is necessary for us to understand that our body was created from the earth. In the earth is found the necessary nutrients that will help our body to heal itself. The prescriptions the doctors give us are not going to heal. Many prescription drugs are synthetic drugs using man-made chemicals rather than natural ingredients. They cover up the symptoms and most of the time give an adverse effect. When that happens, the doctor gives us another prescription to cover up that effect. In turn that gives us another adverse effect and another prescription. It is a vicious circle of destroying our body with no hope of curing it. Seriously, how many older people do we see with bottles and bottles of prescriptions? Yet, there seems to be no healing.

Because I had to learn about natural healing, I kept on the prescriptions for a while after I was discharged from the hospital. I had to do some serious research to comprehend what the Lord wanted me to learn. Once I discovered what to do, I was able to back off the prescriptions. Before long, I was only taking the natural supplements and herbs.

What I am trying to do is encourage Christians to learn to take care of God's temple. We must care for our body as we would our most prized possession. Avoid what is not healthy. Learn about natural supplements. Take prescriptions only as a help until we can depend on the natural supplements from the earth. With the proper nutrients, our body will heal itself. Unless the Lord is calling us home, we can overcome the infirmity in our body. The only other time we'll not be healed is due to a thorn in the flesh. However, that will mean the power of God works mightily in our life like the Apostle Paul, Joni Eareckson Tada, etc.

We must stop indulging in what will only bring our body downhill. It's like allowing the garden to be overcome with weeds. It will strangle the fruit. Well, indulging in fast food, junk food, and an unhealthy diet will strangle our health.

The great thing about God is that after we have done all we can to tend to our body which is his temple, He will give us the supernatural touch needed to bring forth the healing. If we do what is right in his eyes, take in his medicine which is his word to feed our faith, eat healthy, get proper sleep, exercise, etc., He will keep his promise to heal us.

We cannot expect God to heal us when we have neglected his temple. We cannot indulge in what is an unhealthy diet of foods rich in carbohydrates, high-fat content, fried foods, high sodium, etc. and expect to live in health.

An unhealthy or poor nutritious diet can lead to malnutrition, poor digestion, acne, inflammation, osteoarthritis, unwanted weight gain and obesity. It can also increase our risk of chronic diseases, such as diabetes, heart disease, and impact our mental health. We cannot allow ourselves to become obese because of overindulgence and expect not to reap heart disease, stroke, kidney problems, high blood pressure, diabetes, etc.

We reap what we sow (Galatians 6:7). If we sow fast foods, junk food, poor eating habits we will reap an unhealthy body. An unhealthy body is a recipient for all sorts of sickness and disease.

When we yield to the Holy Spirit in us, He will guide us into what we need to take naturally for our body to heal itself. We must adhere to his advice, treat our body like the temple of God it is, and do not defile it in any way by what we eat, drink, etc. We take the natural supplements directed religiously, eat what will help heal, and our body will react positively and heal itself.

If needed after we have done all according to God's will and are standing in supernatural faith, He will supernaturally heal us. God will not always lead us to natural supplements to heal. There are times He will immediately heal us like Paul shaking off the viper into the fire and feeling no harm (Acts 28:5).

If we are the temple of the Holy Ghost, we have been entrusted as caretakers of God's temple. Because it does not belong to us, we have no business defiling, injuring, or abusing it. Whatever we eat or drink is a choice to dishonor or to honor God's temple!

Chapter 9

Stir Up the Gift of God

Wherefore I put thee in remembrance that thou stir up
the gift of God, which is in thee by the putting on of my
hands. For God hath not given us the spirit of fear; but of
power, and of love, and of a sound mind
(2 Timothy 1:6–7).

BEFORE WE CAN COMPREHEND what this book is revealing, we must
realize the Spirit residing in us. It's imperative that we understand
the gift of God dwelling in us. Do we truly comprehend who resides
in us? Do we truly comprehend what He is capable of? Do we truly
comprehend when He speaks, worlds are created?

The real character of Christianity, as it is infused into the soul
of the believer, as it becomes part of us, as it is exhibited in our life
is generally misunderstood. In other words, once the divine nature
becomes part of God's soldier and becomes evidenced in our life, it
is generally misunderstood. Why is that so?

Because it forms a man/woman of energy. It operates like a
new creation. This energy or better called Holy Ghost zeal changes
us to a very considerable extent. Our views, our dispositions, our
habits, our friends, our desires, etc. change so drastically that we no
longer seem to be the same person.

Do we understand that if we, as born again believers, continue to allow the gift of the Holy Spirit in us to have his way, we will be transformed from the image of fallen man (self) into the image of the new man in Christ? We become the image and likeness of Christ Jesus in this world. As Jesus feared nothing, neither does the new man in Christ. Fear will cause unbelief. Unbelief is not faith and will not please God.

In our text there appears to be the implication that Timothy was not letting the Holy Spirit to stir his soul. We sense in the verses that he was afraid and ashamed. It seems he was being influenced by the Jews and false teachers around him. Any time we allow our steadfastness to be influenced by false doctrines, false teachers, or fear, we will find ourselves like Timothy.

How many are not healed or delivered because of being instigating by false teachers? If we allow fear or false teachings to intimidate us, we will neglect our duty. We will be taking in the wrong medicine or fuel that will cause us to sputter or stall. Wrong medicine is like taking in poison that will destroy our faith.

Whether or not Timothy was by his own nature a timid person, the nature of God is one of boldness. We cannot remain what we were before saved. If we were fearful, timid, etc., that person no longer has any authority in our life. We are Christ's and have given our life over to the Holy Spirit to rule (Galatians 2:20).

Let's see if we can give understanding, clarification, illumination as to what God has given to his children. With this comprehension, with more revelation of what we have been given by God, our hearts should be pricked at our lack of faith.

Our constant blurts of frustration, periods of depression, lack of confidence in God, lack of healing, fear of persons or things is really a lack of faith, trust, or belief in God and his ability.

It is actually a lack of faith in the power of our God. Too many times we allow ourselves to be overwhelmed with the problems, the circumstances, the hardships of our life. We have this uncanny ability to LOOK at our problems, our sickness, our lack of finances and turn them into some huge monster about to consume us like Pilgrim or Christian's Giant Despair.

We allow these things to overwhelm us, frighten us, etc. When this happens, we get in such a state of fear and believe the situation will destroy and consume us. We are so busy looking at our self-made mountain, that we can no longer see Christ.

If we kept our eyes on Christ, we would see our mountains are merely mole hills or ant hills in comparison to our God. Only looking at God will keep our thinking in the right perspective.

> Thus saith the Lord, the heaven is my throne, and the earth is my footstool (Isaiah 66:1).

When we truly look at God, we see his greatness, his vastness. Think of the verse in Isaiah. The earth is like a footstool to the immensity of God. How small our problems are to the one who holds the whole earth in his hand (Psalm 95:4).

Why do God's soldiers allow ourselves to be so deceived by self. Why do we allow Satan to deceive us? Why do we insist on concentrating on our problems? Why do we lean on our own understanding? There is only one reason. We do not truly or wholeheartedly trust God, and our faith waivers. Because we don't really know the power of God, we don't comprehend the power that God has endowed us with.

> My people are destroyed for a lack of knowledge (Hosea 4:6).

We are kept so busy with our problems, troubles, tending our sickness, or whatever storm it may be that we neglect the study of God's word. Therefore, we have a lack of knowledge to clothe ourselves in God's supernatural armor that produces supernatural faith that would disable whatever we are facing. Consequently the problems, sickness, lack of finances, etc. destroy us who have the power residing in us to disable, deactivate, or quench the fiery darts of opposition.

Many of God's soldiers were cowards in Christ's day and when things became hard to hear, they walked away (John 6:66). The sad truth is that many of God's soldiers are cowards today who run from the battle when things get tough.

Let me explain that statement. Because of a lack of knowledge, we are overwhelmed by the storms and are quitting. Many of us are running coward from the battle of life and are being overcome and dying.

Some may think using the word *coward* is a strong word. I don't. Let me tell why. If we look at verse seven in our text in 2 Timothy, we see the word *fear* is translated more perfectly as the word *cowardice*.

The scripture is saying that God has *not* given us a Spirit of cowardice. This is fear that creates cowards. It's like the soldier in battle who allows fear to grip him so that he turns and runs away from the fight leaving his comrades to fend for themselves.

God has not nor ever will give us the Spirit that runs from battle. That spirit is not from him. He has given us of his Spirit. The Spirit of God, the Spirit of the Great I Am that I Am dwells within us. God is not and never will be a coward and neither are we to be.

So many times we quote scripture. The Lord doesn't want us to just quote the word, but to live or exhibit it in our lives. We have to understand the words we quote and be strong in the Lord and in the power of his might.

Okay, as we understand and know what God has not given us can help us to realize, to comprehend, to grasp what God has given to us.

First, we're told that God has given us the Spirit of power. To help us realize the Spirit of power, let's make sure we understand the meaning of the spirit of cowardice. Coward is defined as one who lacks courage in the face of danger, pain, or hardship.

We can never walk in the Spirit of power if we allow ourselves to be intimidated or fearful when facing a battle. But God has NOT given us a spirit of cowardice. He has given us the Spirit of power. We don't have to be, nor should we run as cowards. We don't have to be afraid. We have the Spirit of power.

It's imperative that we understand what that POWER is capable of doing or achieving. Once we fully grasp hold of the fact the spirit of cowardice or fear does not come from God, then we are ready to grasp hold of what the Spirit of power means.

Satan wants us ignorant of this scripture. He is aware that if we receive the revelation of what God has given us through the Spirit of power, we are victorious over his wiles, over his lies, over his deceit. The Spirit of power enables us to stand in God's supernatural armor that generates supernatural faith disabling the enemy's fiery darts of sin, sickness, disease, poverty, etc.

> Behold I give unto you power to tread on serpents and scorpions, and over all the power of the enemy: and nothing shall by any means hurt you (Luke 10:19).

Listen to me, Satan cannot overpower us unless we give into a spirit of fear or cowardice. If we stand in the Spirit of power, submit ourselves to God, we resist the devil, and he must flee (James 4:7).

Satan will always get the better of God's soldiers who are in the flesh and not in the Spirit. For a clearer understanding of this truth, my book *Flesh and Spirit Conflict: The Inner Battle of Choice* will illuminate how to overcome or deny our flesh and walk in the Spirit. Only walking in the Spirit will enable us to stand in the Spirit of power that generates supernatural faith disabling all the devil's wiles.

> Watch ye, stand fast in the faith, quit you like men, be strong (1 Corinthians 16:13).

Quit you like men means fight like a man and not a coward. Don't run when the enemy is approaching, but be in watch for him. When he comes, stand strong in the faith, using the full armor of God as our weapons.

As we stand or confront the enemy in the Spirit of power, we are proficient in his weapons. For the weapons, the armaments of our warfare are not carnal, natural, and fleshly, but mighty, supernatural, and spiritual through God to the pulling down of the strongholds or fortresses of Satan (2 Corinthians 10:4).

Now, God has with the Spirit of power given us the Spirit of love. Our love for God, our devotion to Christ causes us to believe in his power, in his ability, in his word.

> There is no fear in love, but perfect love casteth out fear: because fear hath torment (1 John 4:18).

If we are sincerely resting in the love of God, genuinely believing in God's love for us, his perfect love casts out any fear that we may have. We must remember that fear generates unbelief.

This truth is seen in that many times we fear we can't overcome this sin, sickness, disease, habit, poverty, etc. and have torment because we don't really love God or believe He loves us. We allow the spirit of fear to generate unbelief. Only when we love God with all our heart, all our soul, all our strength, and all our mind, will we have complete and total trust in God and have no fear to stand and fight anything that comes our way.

I sense some may misunderstand what to stand and fight means. It doesn't mean to physically by or through physical means to fight. We don't use physical or carnal means. Our weapons are not carnal (natural) but spiritual (supernatural) through God.

The Spirit of power gives us the boldness to be courageous and the Spirit of love makes us willing to do whatever must be done or said.

Now, the Spirit of a sound mind is the Spirit of self-discipline or self-control. That means, we have the ability through the Holy Spirit to discipline ourselves according to the will of God.

> But I keep under my body, and bring it into subjection:
> lest that by any means, when I have preached to others,
> I myself should become a castaway (1 Corinthians 9:27).

We have the power of self-control, the power to keep our whole being in subjection to the Lord. We have the power to control what we eat or drink. We have the power to eat healthy and allow our bodies to be in health.

We have the power to keep ourselves separated from the world and its evil powers. We have, because of God's love, the power to regulate our lives in accordance to the word of God which is the will of God. We have the power to believe God or believe the lie.

If we stir up the gift of God in us, the Spirit of a sound mind will enable us to deny our flesh that wants to become a coward during the battle. The Spirit of love will force us through the Spirit of power to stand and fight in God's spiritual or supernatural armor enabling spiritual or supernatural faith to rise up in us and disable whatever fiery dart Satan has hurled at us.

Now, how do we know we are standing in God's armor? We know we are standing in his supernatural armor when we believe God and his word. We have no unbelief, doubt, fear, etc. We know God is all-powerful, all-knowing, everywhere present, and will never change.

When we stir up the gift of the Holy Ghost in us, we comprehend it's not faith in what we know or what we have learned. Supernatural faith stands in God's supernatural armor believing in his power and ability. It knows who God is and what *his* faith is capable of doing.

Let me help us understand how to disable or quench all fiery darts. As we read about Israel, we see they had many mighty deliverances. Yet, when they allowed their mind, their thoughts, their faith to go into the wilderness of unbelief, they spent forty years walking away from the promise.

To receive the promise, we must keep our mind, our thoughts, our faith centered on the promise and our mind, our thoughts, our faith out of the wilderness of unbelief. If we focus on the promise, we will disable or quench the fiery darts. If we believe the evil report, we will spend our life in the wilderness of unbelief walking away from the promise.

Supernatural faith disables, quenches, annihilates all fiery darts of unbelief, doubt, fear, anxiety, sickness, disease, etc. When we stand in God's supernatural faith, his supernatural armor is indestructible and what He has promised will be manifested!